Payment card domain knowledge

Card terminology, processing & security in PCI (Payment Card Industry)

Dedicated to all the software professionals.

Author information

For any help please contact :

Amazon Author Page : amazon.com/author/ajaykumar
Email : ajaycucek@gmail.com , ajaxreso@gmail.com
Linkedin : https://www.linkedin.com/in/ajaycucek
Facebook : https://www.facebook.com/ajaycucek
Youtube :
https://www.youtube.com/channel/UC1uXEebtqCLYxVdzirK
ZGIA
Twitter : https://twitter.com/ajaycucek
Instagram : https://www.instagram.com/ajaycucek/
Skype : ajaycucek

Table of contents

5

..

.

Book Overview

Book Overview

This book "Payment card domain knowledge
Card terminology, processing & security in PCI (Payment Card
Industry)" includes all the information of PCI (Payment Card
Industry). So we're going to find out how a transaction that you
make in-store or online, how that appears on your payment card
statements. We're going to look at the data messages exchanged
between all the participants in the payment system, and then
discover how criminals can take these messages, steal them, and
turn them into money. Some of the major topics that we'll cover
include: what payment card data moves around the world, what's
the point of all the different PCI standards, who cares whether
you are compliant, which assessor to use to validate your
compliance, how to become a PCI professional. By the end of this
book, you will understand how the PCI standards are designed to
protect payment card data from criminals. There are no
pre-requisites, and from here, you'll be more confident working
on payments and PCI projects.

Module 1 : Discovering How Card Payments Work

How Payment Card Transactions Appear on a Statement

Card Statement
4687 38** **** 7980

Pizza	$13.20
Rail fare	$56.87
Wired Brain Coffee	$ 5.10
Plu	$29.99
Web hosting	$ 9.99
Total	$115.15

Have you ever wondered how when you make a transaction using your payment card, such as buying a cup of coffee, it appears on your bank statement, or card statement, a few days later? Let's see how that works.

"I'll have a large latte to go, please"   "That will be $5.10"   "I'll pay by card..."   "Here you go"

Imagine, Ann Cardholder goes into her favorite Wired Brain coffee shop and asks for a latte. The assistant, Wanda, asks Ann for $5. 10. Ann decides that she wants to pay by card. She either swipes the magnetic stripe, dips the chip, or taps for a contact list transaction, and receives a delicious latte from Wanda.

What Are People Thinking?

Wanda Wired-Brain

Will I get paid?

Ann Cardholder

Can I have that latte?

Ann's Bank

Is this really Ann, or is it fraud?

Does Ann have enough cash or credit?

So what are all the participants in the transaction really thinking when Ann uses her card? Wanda is concerned that if she lets Ann walk out the store with the latte, whether Wired Brain coffee will get paid for it. Ann is just hoping that the transaction works okay because she really wants that latte, and she didn't bring any cash with her. Ann's bank is wondering if it really is Ann making the transaction or if it is someone pretending to be Ann, and also, whether Ann has enough money in her account or enough credit to afford the $5. 10.

The Purpose of Authorization

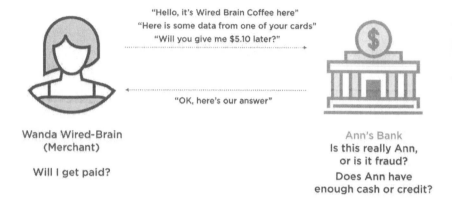

"Hello, it's Wired Brain Coffee here"
"Here is some data from one of your cards"
"Will you give me $5.10 later?"

"OK, here's our answer"

Wanda Wired-Brain
(Merchant)

Will I get paid?

Ann's Bank
Is this really Ann,
or is it fraud?
Does Ann have
enough cash or credit?

The first step in payment processing, authorization, answers both Wanda's and the bank's question. Now the proper term for an organization that accepts payment cards is a merchant. So basically Wanda, the merchant, sends an electronic message to the bank. This message contains the data from Ann's payment card, and asks the bank, if Wanda lets Ann walk out with a latte now, will the bank give Wired Brain Coffee the $5. 10 later? Based on the information that the merchant sends, the bank works out two things. Firstly, whether it believes it really is Ann making the transaction or if it's someone pretending to be Ann. So the bank will check to see if the card being used has been reported lost or stolen, and it will probably make some other checks, such as if it thinks Ann is in the same country as the merchant, or if she's bought coffee there before. The bank will also check to make sure that Ann actually has $5. 10 in her account or within her credit limit, and if the bank is happy that it really is Ann and that she has enough money, it will send a message back to the merchant saying that it's okay to let Ann have that latte, and the bank will pay the merchant later. This is called authorization.

The Purpose of Authorization

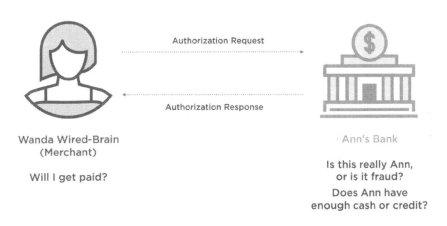

Authorization Request

Authorization Response

Wanda Wired-Brain
(Merchant)

Will I get paid?

Ann's Bank

Is this really Ann,
or is it fraud?

Does Ann have
enough cash or credit?

The message from the merchant to the bank is known as an authorization request, and the message sent back from the bank to the merchant is called the authorization response. Authorization responses are usually authorized, but if the bank isn't happy because it thinks, well the transaction's fraudulent, and or the cardholder doesn't have sufficient funds, it could also be declined, and in that case, Ann wouldn't have got her latte. So authorization's the first step in any payment card transaction. Ann has a latte, and Wired Brain Coffee has a promise from the bank that it will receive $5. 10 in the future.

Steps in the Transaction

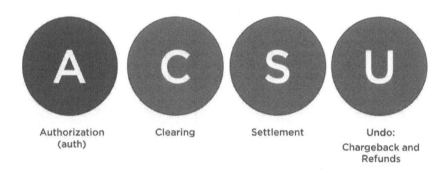

We're going to look in more detail at authorization and the other steps in the payment process: Clearing and settlement, which are how Wired Brain Coffee will receive the $5. 10, and the two ways of undoing a transaction: chargebacks and refunds. And the reason why we're doing this is because in each of these steps, some data moves around the system; in the merchant's network and in the bank's network, and the key to payment security is knowing where to find that data, knowing what's in the data, and therefore, how it needs to be protected.

The Data Stored on a Payment Card

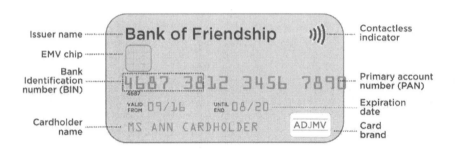

Although all payment cards use different logos and colors, they all the same data elements on them, and they're usually always in the same place on the card. So let's find out where the data is on a payment card. Starting on the front, there will always be the name of the card issuer, typically a bank, or a card scheme. Some cards will have this funny symbol that looks like ripples, which says the card can be used with contactless transactions, and lots of cards now contain a smart EMV chip, that helps make transactions more secure. Now we get to the data that's normally embossed on a card. Across the middle of the card is the 15 or 16-digit card number, or as the payment industry calls it, the primary account number, or PAN. The first six digits of the

PAN are special because they are unique to each bank and are balled the bank identification number, or BIN. Some cards will have a valid from or start date, but all will have an expiration date, after which time, the card is no longer valid. Depending on which bank issued the card, this could be labeled as valid till, or until end, or just expiration date. The cardholder's name will be there, and finally, a logo from the card brand, American Express, Discover, JCB, MasterCard, or Visa.

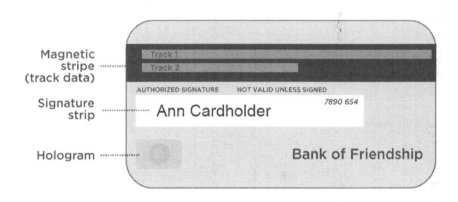

Turning to the back of the card, there's a lot less here. The magnetic stripe contains all the data on the front of the card, and more, in a digital form that can be read by a merchant's equipment. It actually contains a couple of data formats known as tracks, that a merchant's systems know how to read. These are brilliantly called Track 1 and Track 2. Although the magnetic stripe's usually black or dark brown, some manufacturers have tried really hard to make an attractive silver or gold magnetic stripe. So it might not look like a magnetic stripe, it might look like decoration, but it's always going to be there in the same physical place on the card. There'll be a signature strip so when the cardholder signs a receipt, the merchant will be able to compare the signature on the receipt with the one on the card. Yeah, I know merchants never actually physically check signatures anymore, but that's what the signature strip's for, and finally, most cards will contain a hologram, so the merchant can look at the card and check it to make sure it isn't a forgery.

Cardholder Data: Track 1

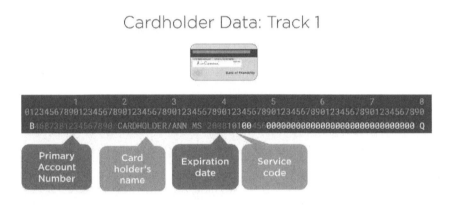

Now looking in a bit more detail at the magnetic stripe on the back of the card, we said it contains two tracks of data. They're called Track 1 and Track 2. The first track, Track 1, is 80 characters long, and it contains the primary account number, the cardholder name, the expiration date, and a service code that says what sort of card it is, and you can see those numbers there encoded on the magnetic stripe.

Sensitive Authentication Data (SAD)

What's also there is some data that's used in the authentication process to prove the card is real. This is called sensitive authentication data, it's data that's sent by the merchant to the issuer that says if I've got this data, it's probably more likely than not that I've got the real card. There can be two types of sensitive authentication data on Track 1. Firstly, the secret three digit number that's not printed anywhere on the card, that only the issuing bank also knows. Annoyingly, each card brand has a different name for this. Visa calls it the card verification value or CVV, MasterCard calls it the card verification code or CVC. You'll see both written down quite commonly, I'm going to stick for CVV for most of this. There's also another value in there which is used to validate pins called the pin verification value or PVV. I've not shown any of what might be after the card verification value.

Basically, the rule is that anything from the card verification value onwards, that the issuer of the card can do with what they want. So it's usually got CVV in there, it's usually got a PVV in there, and this is quite important, because there's some rules in PCI DSS that say what data a merchant can store,

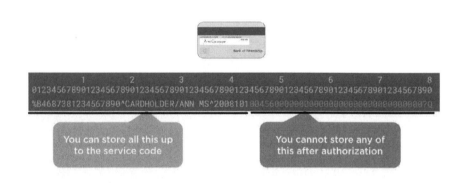

and so basically, any of the information you see there above black underlined , so that's the service code, and to the left of the service code, the merchant can store any time they want. Why they do that, we're going to talk about later and whether that's a good idea. Basically, anything to the right of the service code, so all the stuff that's shown in black underlined, but I've just shown lots of zeros, because again, that's up to the issuer. Anything to the right of the service code can't be stored by the merchant after authorization.

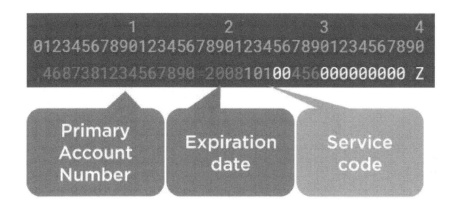

If we look at the other track, Track 2, it's much shorter. It's just 40 characters, and again, you'll see it contains the primary account number, the expiration date, and the service code. Again, to the right of the service code is information that will be used by the card issuer,

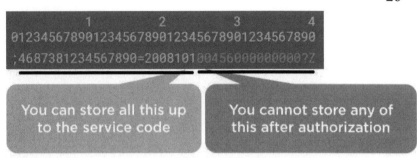

and just as before, you can't store any of that after authorization. There's typically going to be the CVV, the card verification value in there.

The Entities Involved in Authorizing a Payment Card Transaction

What data is present on the card

What the merchant's systems can read

So remember, that the aim of authorization is to read the data from the customer's card, and send it to an issuing bank. How the data's read from the card depends on where you are in the world. Both in how the data is actually stored on the card and actually what date is available, and the technical capabilities of the merchant to read the card. There are three ways the merchant may accept the transaction. If it's a mag stripe transaction, the merchant could swipe it through the point of sale system, through a dedicated card reader, or through a payment device. In an EMV, or chip market, the merchant will insert the card into an EVM reader, and in a contactless transaction, the cardholder would just tap their card onto the card reader. In all three types of transactions, information is being read from the card into the merchant systems. That information will be then used by the merchant to make an authorization request. Let's start with a mag stripe transaction. We'll look at EVM or chip transactions in a later module.

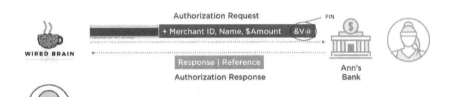

So equipment at the merchant reads the entire Track 1 data from the card and sends it along with information about the merchant, the amount of transaction, and possibly an encrypted value based on the pin, to the issuing bank. This is called the authorization request. The cardholder's issuing bank checks the data, determines if it's a real or a fraudulent transaction, and also whether there are sufficient funds or credit to allow the transaction to take place, and then it will send an authorization response to the merchant, which typically consists of a response such as accept or decline, and a reference number or code to identify that the merchant received a response.

Authorization in Practice

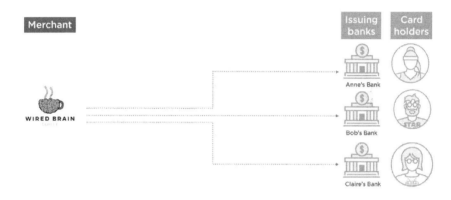

Now for this process to happen, the merchant, Wide Brain Coffee, would have to have relationships with every bank in the world that issued payment cards, just in case one of that bank's customers came into their coffee shop, and that's just too many relationships in contrast for every single merchant to have.

Authorization in Practice

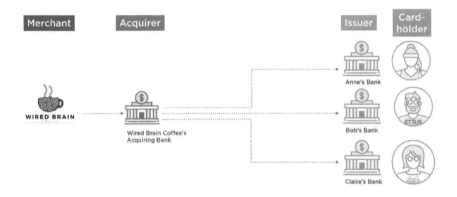

So what happens in practice is that every merchant that accepts payment cards has a relationship with an acquiring bank, that's a bank that acquires their payment card transactions, and it's this acquiring bank that builds relationships with every card issuing bank in the world.

Authorization in Practice

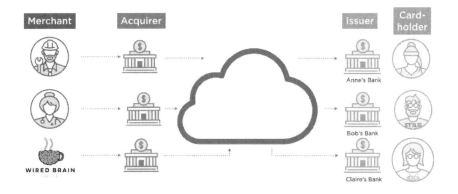

Of course, even this would be massively complicated. There are hundreds of acquiring banks, and if each one had to build relationships and agree separate contracts with every single issuing bank, they'd also drown in paperwork and lawyers.

Authorization in Practice

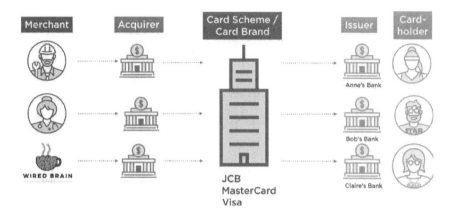

So there has to be something in the middle that connects all the acquiring banks with all the issuing banks, and that something is the card schemes or as PCI calls them, card brands: Visa, MasterCard, and JCB. They connect all the acquiring banks with all the card issuing banks. So what really happens in our example authorization is that the authorization request goes from Wide Brain Coffee to Wide Brain's acquiring bank, and then to the card scheme, such as Visa or MasterCard. The card scheme then sends the authorization request to Ann's issuing bank, and then waits for the authorization response from the bank that issued the card to Ann, so it can then send the response to Wired Brain's acquirer. Now, here's probably one of the most important things to know about the payment industry. Although it is full of standards and rules, because it covers the whole world, there are lots of differences in the way that the system works. Those differences can be because of the country you're in, because of local laws, historical ways that payments have worked in a certain region, there are all sorts of reasons, and so although most of the general principles of this course will be valid, you will always find some differences in the places where you work. There's no universal way that every single payment happens everywhere in the world, but that's actually what makes this industry really interesting to work in.

Four-party Model

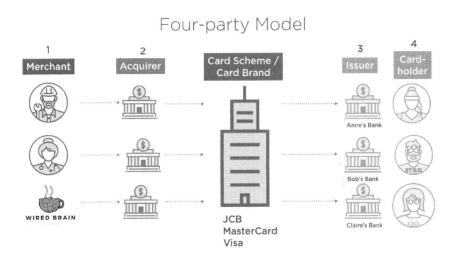

And our first irregularity is that actually not all card payments work in the way that we've just shown, in what's called a four-party model where there's a merchant, an acquirer, an issuer, and a cardholder. Another way that payments very often work is what's called the three-party model,

Three-party Model

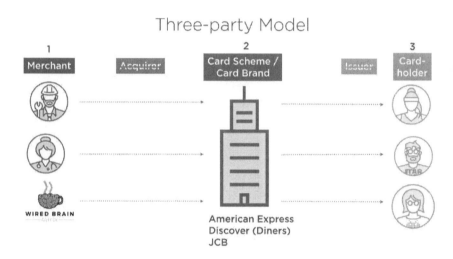

American Express
Discover (Diners)
JCB

where there's no acquiring bank or issuing bank. The card scheme gives cards directly to cardholders, and develops relationships directly with merchants to acquire their transactions. An example of card schemes that are basically third-party schemes are American Express and Discover, and in some parts of the world you'll also hear Discover being called Diners, and JCB also works in this three-party model, as well as in the four-party model. Now, whether it's a three-party scheme, or a four-party scheme, at the end of authorization, the merchant has a promise to pay from the cardholder's bank, or in a three-party scheme, the card issuer, and the cardholder has their coffee. The next step is to discover how the merchant actually gets their real money.

Getting Paid: Clearing and Settlement

The steps in the payment process that mean the merchant actually gets paid are called clearing and settlement.

Clearing (4-party)

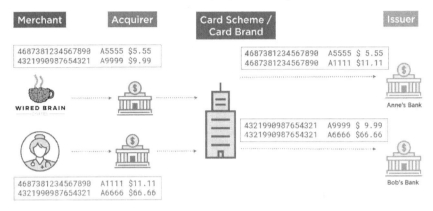

In clearing, each merchant sends a summary of all their day's transactions to their acquirer. This will typically just contain the primary account numbers of the card used to make the transaction, the authorization reference, and the amounts. None of the other data that we use for authorization, such as the full track data, will be included in the clearing message, and this is important because authorization messages contain more data than clearing messages. Each acquirer then splits every merchant's transactions out into each card scheme, and I've just shown one scheme here to make it easy to follow. The scheme works out which transaction is for which issuing bank, and it does this based on the first six digits of the PAN, which you'll remember is the bank identification number, and it sends all the transactions for each issuing bank together.

Settlement (4-party)

| Merchant | Acquirer | Card Scheme / Card Brand | Issuer |

$16.66

$15.54

WIRED BRAIN

Anne's Bank

$77.77

$76.65

Bob's Bank

The issuing bank then work out how much money they owe to the card scheme for every transaction included in the day's clearing data, and they send it to the card scheme. This is called settlements. The scheme then sends this onto the acquiring banks, which separate it out, and send the money to the merchants. Some merchants get their funds the next day, whereas others might wait a few days or even a month before receiving their money. This is all based on the agreement between the merchant and their acquiring bank, and is mostly dependent on the sort of goods or services the merchant sells, and how long the merchant's been in business.

Clearing (3-party)

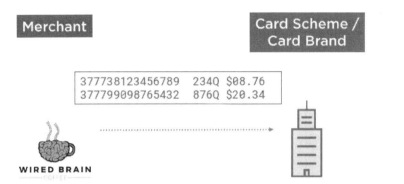

Now, for clearing in a three-party scheme, remember there's no acquirer, and there's no issuing bank, so the merchants send a summary of all their day's transactions directly to the scheme,

Settlement (3-party)

Merchant

Card Scheme /
Card Brand

$29.10

WIRED BRAIN

and then the scheme settles the money out to the merchant for all the transactions.

Irregularities

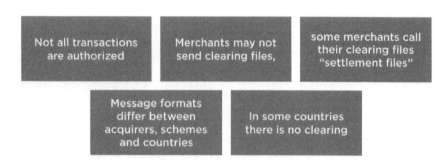

Now, remember what we said about irregularities in the payment system? Well, this is really noticeable in authorization, clearing, and settlements. Firstly, not all transactions are authorized. Depending on the amount of the transaction, and sometimes how the transaction is made, there may not be an authorization request. Sometimes a merchant will just choose to trust they will get paid once they've captured the cardholder's data. Often a merchant won't send a clearing file. The acquirer, or the scheme will work this out for them, and even if the merchant does make a clearing file, sometimes you'll hear them refer to it or call it a settlement file. The message formats and the contents of the messages between acquirers, merchants, and schemes differs between different acquirers in different countries, and in different payment schemes, and in some countries there is actually no clearing, settlement is always worked out just from the authorization request. But whatever happens, there will, at a minimum, be one message that leaves the merchants and will contain sufficient cardholder data for the issuer to debit the cardholder and to send the money to the merchants.

E-commerce Transactions and Payment Service Providers

In an e-commerce transaction, which you'll also hear called a customer not present, or CNP transaction, there are the same authorization, clearing, and settlement steps in the payment process. So let's imagine that our cardholder Ann wants to buy some coffee beans using her payment card from the Wired Bean Coffee website.

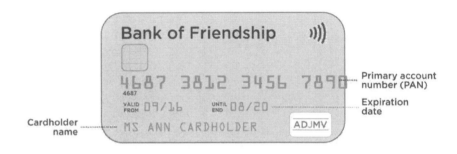

The information Ann will need is printed on her payment card. The PAN, the expiration date, and her name as it's printed on the card,

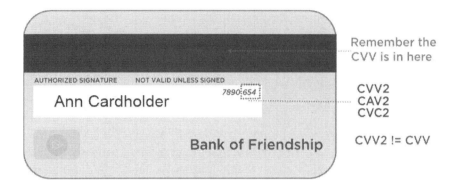

and if we turn the card over, the security code printed on the back of the card, which, just like the security code that's encoded on the magnetic stripe, is called different things by each card scheme. I'm generally going to call it the card verification value 2, or CVV2, that's what Visa calls it, MasterCard calls it the CVC2. So, it's important to know this three digit value is different to the CVV value encoded on the magnetic stripe. That way, if a criminal steals data from a website, they won't have the CVV value from the magnetic stripe, they'll just have the CVV2 value, and so they can't make a clone card, and similarly, if a criminal steals data from a point of sale system, they won't have the CVV2 data, so they can't go shopping on the internet. Visa, MasterCard, Discover, and JCB all print their three-digit security code on the signature strip on the back of the card. American Express has a four-digit security code, which they call CID< and this is printed on the front of an AMEX card, just to the right of, or just below the embossed primary account number. Now the steps in an e-com transaction are generally the same as they are in a normal transaction: authorization, clearing, and settlement, but there's another irregularity with e-commerce that you'll see a lot, which is a step called capture. It sort of sits after the authorization step, and it's used because there's a delay between the merchant accepting an e-com transaction, and the goods actually being sent to the customer. Capture's not there in every single e-commerce implementation, it depends how the acquirer works with the merchant, and what the merchant does.

E-commerce Authorization

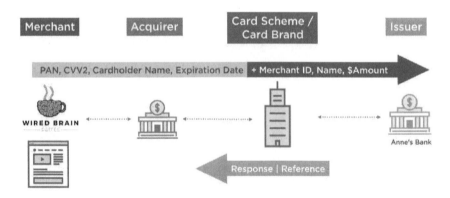

So let's have a look at e-com authorization. In a typical e-com authorization, the cardholder enters their data into the merchant website. This data, consisting of PAN, CVV2, cardholder name and expiration date, is sent, along with the merchant's details and the amount of the transaction, to the issuing bank for authorization, and just as with a face- to-face transaction, the merchant's going to receive an authorization response message from the issuing bank.

E-commerce Capture

In some cases, and remember this doesn't happen for all e-com transactions, there will be a delay between when the customer orders the goods or services, and when they are dispatched by the merchants. If this is the case, the merchant often makes an arrangement that as well as sending the authorization request when the customer places their order, the merchant will also send a capture request to the acquirer to confirm the transaction's really happening, and the merchant's fulfilled their side of the contract. This capture transaction will typically just include the PAN and a reference.

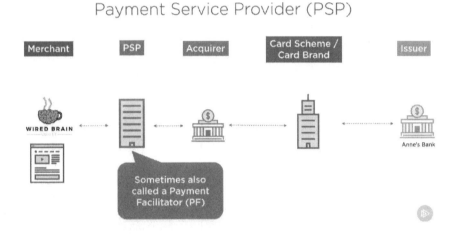

Often in an e-commerce transaction, you'll find another third-party involved that sits between the merchant and their acquirer: a payment service provider, or PSP. They can be used by all sizes of merchants, and in the early days of e-commerce, payment service providers were the people who worked out how to make card payments happen on the internet. Nowadays, you'll often see payment service providers also called payment facilitators, or PFs.

Payment Service Provider (PSP)

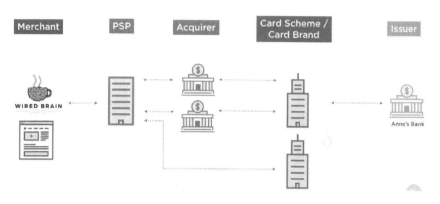

A PSP can make it really easy for small merchants to start selling on the internet because the PSP takes care of all the complicated paperwork with the acquires and the card schemes. PSPs can also be valuable for really large merchants to use because they just have one interface to the PSP, and then they can say to the PSP, route this transaction to one acquirer, route a different transaction to another acquirer, and then route this transaction straight to a card scheme, and so they can get independence from acquirers, which helps them in terms of negotiating better rates from certain acquirers with perhaps different types of transactions or different currencies. So you see a PSP used by all sizes of merchants. In e-commerce transactions, clearing a settlement happens, just in the same way as it does in a face-to-face transaction. Clearing files go from merchants to acquirers, from acquirers to schemes, and then to the issuing banks, and settlement money goes in the other direction back to the merchants.

Undoing a Transaction: Refunds and Chargebacks

So far, we've discovered how merchants authorize transactions and get paid. We've also found out that the data contained in the authorization and clearing messages is what the issuing bank uses to make sure a transaction will appear on a cardholder statement, but what happens when things go wrong? When a transaction ends up on the wrong cardholder's account? When the cardholder takes something back to the merchant because they changed their mind, or they were not happy? There needs to be a way to undo payment card transactions. There are two ways a transaction can be undone.

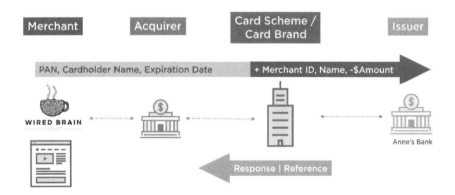

Refund: Merchant Initiates

Firstly, the merchant can refund the transaction. To do this, the merchant sends a message similar to an authorization request to the cardholder's bank. Unlike an authorization request, this refund message doesn't usually contain the sensitive authentication data the issuer required for authorization, just the PAN, cardholder name, and expiration date, along with the amount being refunded to the cardholder, and as you'd expect, the issuer will send back a refund response.

Refund: Merchant Initiates

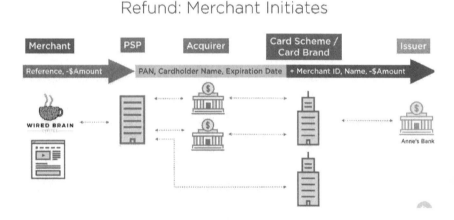

But if the merchant is using a payment service provider, this can often make refunds even easier because the merchant just needs to send the PSP transaction reference, and the amount to the PSP, which will then generate the necessary messages to send to the issuing bank. Remember, a refund is initiated by the merchant.

Chargeback: Cardholder Initiates

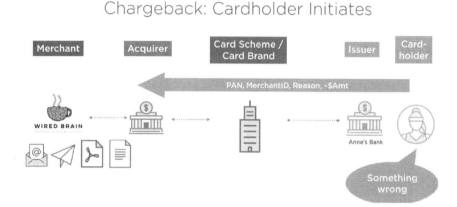

Transactions can also be undone by the cardholder contacting their bank and stating that either the transaction on their account was not them but fraud, or that the merchant didn't fulfill its contract with the cardholder. This type of transaction is called a chargeback. The cardholder will first contact their issuing bank to say something is wrong. They'll usually have to complete a form, and then the issuing bank sends a message via the card scheme to the merchant's acquirer, requesting that the money is returned. This message will specify the reason and might also contain a copy of the form the cardholder completed. The acquirer will contact the merchant and ask them to prove the transaction was valid, and I've seen this can happen in many different ways: by fax, by email, by post, and quite commonly today the acquirer makes a website available for their merchants, and the merchant can then log in and see all the chargebacks. If the merchant agrees to the chargeback, the transaction is undone. If the merchant disagrees, a dispute process starts, which is eventually decided by the card scheme if neither the issuing bank or the acquiring bank can agree. From a data perspective, this dispute happens between the banks. The merchant doesn't really get involved in this, and at a merchant you will find chargeback letters, faxes, and emails from the acquirer, but these have tended to be sent over separate channels, separate manual channels quite frequently, from the system that is used to authorize and clear transactions.

Getting Cash from an ATM

Now let's not forget that there are lots of transactions made
every day by cash and not by card; however, these often start as a
card transaction at an automated teller machine or ATM, where
the cardholder uses their payment card to withdraw cash from
their accounts.

Cash Authorization

These transactions are really similar to the retail transactions
we've already seen. Once the cardholder puts their card into an
ATM, an authorization request is going to go from the bank that

operates the ATM to the cardholder's issuing bank. Sometimes this goes by one of the card schemes, and sometimes it just gets sent from one bank to another, and in some countries, there's a national equivalent to the card scheme just for ATM transactions, but just as with a payment transaction, once the transaction has been authorized, the cardholder's bank will send a response to the bank that runs the ATM, which if the response is okay, it means the ATM will be instructed to dispense the cash to the cardholder. At the end of the day, the ATM bank will produce a clearing file and will get settlements early the next day.

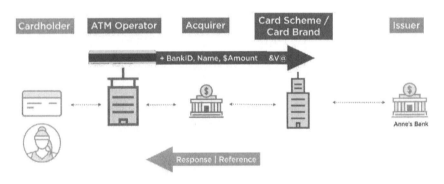

Cash Authorization – ATM Operators

In some cases, rather than the ATM being run by a bank, they're run by third-party companies. So the authorization message goes from the ATM to the ATM operator, and to an acquirer, just like in a retail transaction, and then the settlement comes back the next day in the same sort of way.

Summary of How Payment Transactions Work

We started off this module asking how when you made a payment transaction, the transaction was shown on your account or credit card statement, and the money left your account.

Issuing banks (ISSUERS) and CARD SCHEMES (3-party) provide cards to CARDHOLDERS

Acquiring banks (ACQUIRERS) and card schemes (3 party) acquire transactions from MERCHANTS

Card schemes (4 party) connect acquirers to issuers

PAYMENT SERVICE PROVIDERS (PSP) and PAYMENT FACILTATORS (PF) contract with merchants to send the transactions to acquirers

To find out how this works, we've met all the participants in the payment process. Issuing banks and three-party card schemes, such as AMEX and Discover that give payment cards to individual cardholders. Acquiring banks and three-party card schemes that accept transactions from merchants. Card schemes that join acquiring banks to issuing banks in a four-party model, commonly Visa and MasterCard. and payment service providers, or payment facilitators that can sit between merchants and acquiring banks. We discovered that there are a number of steps in the payment process, and that each of the steps in the electronic message will be sent between the participants. It is the contents of these messages that make transactions happen. Each of these messages contain data, and understanding the purpose of each message, and what data it will contain is the first step in knowing how to protect this data from criminal theft or manipulation.

In AUTHORIZATION, the merchant checks with the issuing bank that they will be paid

In CAPTURE, a merchant confirms the transaction has taken place

In CLEARING, merchants and acquirers summarize their daily transactions, issuers debit the cardholder account

In SETTLEMENT, issuers transfer money to acquirers and the acquirer pays the merchant

A merchant can REFUND a transaction

A cardholder can CHARGEBACK a transaction (via their issuer)

The first step in the payment process is authorization, which happens when the customer starts the transaction. The merchant wants to make sure they will get paid, and it is an authorization message that contains the most data. In some cases, the merchant also has to capture a transaction by confirming they have completed their part of the contract with the customer. After authorization, clearing messages are exchanged so that all parties know how much they owe each other at the end of the day, and then settlement happens where the money moves from the banks that issue cards to the merchants. Finally, we learned that transactions can be undone, either by a merchant issuing a refund to a cardholder, or a cardholder stating that they didn't make a transaction, and initiating a chargeback. And finally, I'd like to remind you that the world is a very big place. The payment system has been developed over about 50 years. It started out with bits of paper being posted from merchants to acquirers, acquirers to schemes, and schemes to issuing banks. Over time this has moved to electronic processing. Some payment systems started out in their own countries, and they were built to different standards to other country systems. It's really been only in the last what, 20 years or so that the entire global payment system has been properly electronically connected. This means that different countries, acquirers, and schemes can work in their own individual ways. So although everything we've talked about here is generally what happens, you will always find variations, but in almost all cases, for a merchant to get paid, there will be messages sent from the merchant to the acquirer service provider or card scheme, which will end up at an issuing bank. Finding out what's in these messages, where they go, and how they get there is the secret to securing payments.

Module 2 : Working Out Which PCI Standards Apply

How Criminals Profit from Payment Card Data

Hi. In this module, we're going to discover all the different PCI standards, and which ones could apply to what you do. But firstly, have you ever wondered how criminals turn stolen card data into cash? They do this in two ways: either by taking stolen cardholder data and using that data to create clone cards that they can use to get cash out of ATMs, or by buying goods in shops with clone cards and selling those goods for cash, or buying stuff online with stolen card data and selling those things that they've bought for cash. Typically, it's not just one criminal involved in turning card data into money. There are usually at least four criminals involved. The first criminal specializes in stealing card data from companies. The second criminal is a data dealer. They find people to sell the data to. The third criminal works out how to turn the data they have bought into money. They may create clone cards or shop online and recruit people to have goods shipped to them that can then be forwarded to the criminal and turned into cash. And the final criminal is known as the mule, and it's the job of the mule to actually turn it to cash over stolen goods. They may have to go to lots of ATM machines to make withdrawals, or go shopping online and then ship the stolen goods to the criminal number three, or even go shopping in store, and ship the goods to the criminal number three, or pass them to someone else who will make money from it. Quite often the mule is not a real criminal, but someone who's been recruited for a work at home scheme on the internet. They may think they have a job as a parcel forwarder, but what they're really doing is resending goods that have been purchased with stolen payment card data. It is often the mules who are most easily caught because they have parcels shipped to their real address, and so law enforcement could also go to the mule's real address. Now, let's look at the data a criminal might need to steal.

Cash

Typically cash out at an Automated Teller Machine (ATM)

Requires clone magnetic stripe card
- Track 1

PIN

To get cash, criminals want to visit an ATM. They need to make clone cards to use in the ATM, so they need to get the entire contents of Track 1 data from the magnetic stripe, and they also need to have somehow capture the cardholder's PIN. To get physical goods, the criminal has two options:

Physical goods

In-store (face-to-face, customer present)
- Clone magnetic stripe card
  - Track 1

E-commerce (customer not present)
- PAN, expiration date, name
- CVV2 (not always requested)
- Billing address

they could visit a physical store, in which case they'll need clone magnetic stripe data using the Track 1 data they've stolen from somewhere else, or they can make an e-commerce transaction, so they will just require the data that's used to authorize an e-commerce transaction, which is PAN, expiration date, and the cardholder's name, and they may need to the CVV2 security code, although not all merchants ask for this. And some e-commerce merchants will also check the cardholder's billing address with the card issuer as part of the authorization message. As we discovered in the previous module, there are four possible steps in a payment card transaction where the data moves between merchants, banks, and card schemes: authorization, clearing, settlement, and the undo transactions: chargebacks and refunds. The authorization step is the one that contains the most data, as this is the step where the issuer works out if they want to authorize a transaction, and so this step had to contain all the data that the issuer needs. So logically, if a criminal steals authorization data, then the criminal has all the data needed to make a criminal authorization request. If we look at authorization data for the various different ways that card data is accepted,

Track 1

- ATM or
- In-store
- Fuel, Ticketing etc

PAN+Exp+CVV2

- E-commerce
- Mail Order / Telephone Order (MOTO)

PAN+Exp

- All Track 1 data
- E-commerce or MOTO

criminals need Track 1 data to get cash from an ATM and goods from physical stores, and they can steal Track 1 data from ATMs, or from retail stores, and also other places where the magnetic stripe is swiped, such as fuel dispensers and transport ticketing machines. Now, I know as well as Track 1 data, criminals need PINs to get cash from ATMs, and we're going to look at how criminals steal PINs a bit later because it's not possible to steal a PIN just by stealing data from the authorization request. To make e-commerce and mail order transactions, criminals just need to steal the PAN, expiration date, and CVV2 from other e-commerce or mail order and telephone order retailers. The payment industry uses the term MOTO, M-O-T-O, for mail order, telephone order retailers, and in some cases, if the criminals find an e-commerce or MOTO retailer that doesn't even check the CVV2 security code, they can use any source of PAN and expiration date, which includes both track data and the data taken from e-commerce websites. Much face-to-face fraud is stopped by chip cards, but until chip cards are everywhere in the world, criminals will still target magnetic stripe transactions. So let's find out how criminals use stolen mag stripe data first, and then later, we'll look at the difference that chip technology makes.

Where to Find Data Worth Stealing

So now we know what data criminals want to steal, let's see where they can find this data. Now you'll remember, that to authorize a face-to-face transaction, the whole of the magnetic stripe is sent to the issuing bank, and so if a criminal can take a copy of this data, they'll be able to make a clone card by writing the magnetic stripe data they steal from a merchant onto a blank card, and the issuing bank won't know the difference between the real card and the clone card, and would authorize transactions from both.

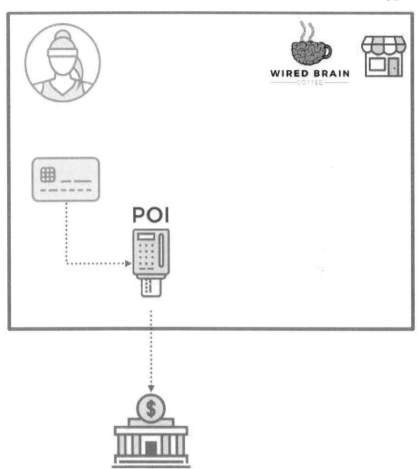

Looking at a simple retail example, the card could be read in a dedicated card terminal, which in the payment industry is called a point of interaction, or POI. You'll also hear these referred to as PIN entry devices, or PEDs. So it could be sent from this device straight to the acquiring bank.

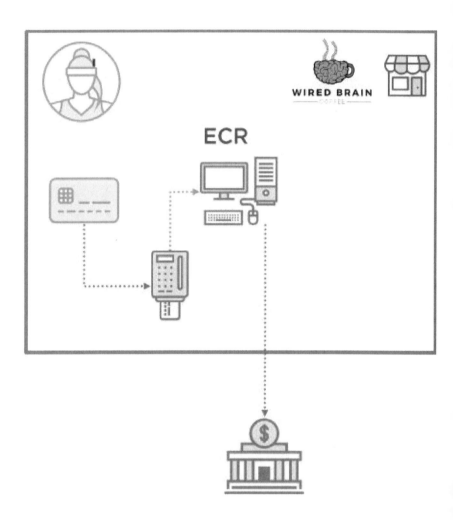

On the other hand, the data can flow from the point of interaction into the merchant's cash register, which you'll also often see called an ECR, or some people call it a POS, a point of sale, and then it goes from the ECR directly to the acquirer.

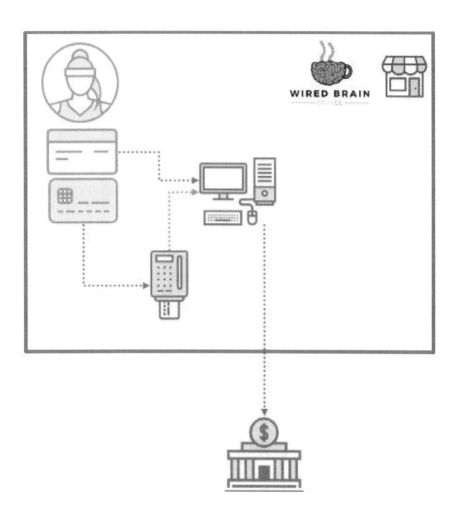

If the merchant's traditionally accepted magnetic stripe transactions, the card might even be swiped through a reader attached to the keyboard in the ECR. So as before, the ECR can communicate directly with the acquirer, or a POI device could send the data through the ECR and then to the acquirer.

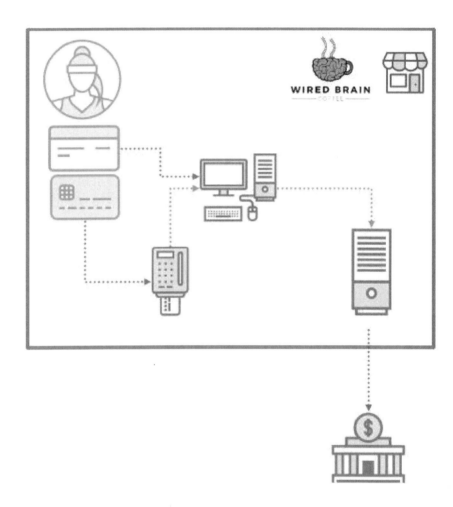

And in many cases, they'll be a central server or controller in each merchant's store, so all the transactions are consolidated into one place from all cash registers before they get sent to an acquirer.

Where to Find Authorization Data (Face-to-face)

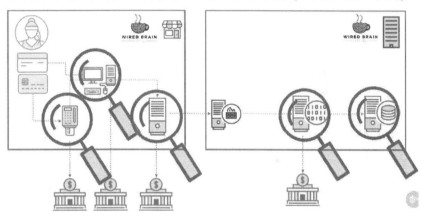

Of course, like Wired Brain Coffee, many retailers have got more than one store or physical location, and so you can also find that authorization messages pass through from each store to a head office system where they get sent to an acquirer. And so in some cases, you'll even see a hybrid, where the authorization's requested locally from the server in a retail store, but it's also passed through to the head office servers just in case. So if the store authorization system fails, transactions can be authorized by going via head office, and of course, sometimes head office saves this data just in case, or keeps it for later processing, for example, to create clearing files. And so depending on how the merchant gets the authorization message from the card to the merchant's acquiring bank, you could find authorization data here, or here on the ECR, or here in a store server, or here in head office at something like a payment server or a payment switch, or even here in a database.

Where to Find Authorization Data (E-commerce)

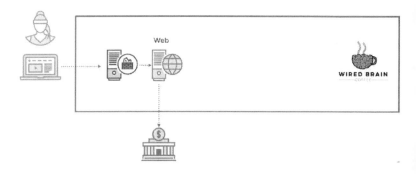

In e-commerce, you'll also find differences in the way the authorization data gets from the time that the consumer enters it into the web browser to the acquirer. The simplest, shown here is that one's payment data is received by Wired Brain Coffee's web server is sent directly from the web server to the acquirer. In some larger merchants you'll tend to find they've got multiple web servers with say, load balancers in front of them, which means sometimes you'll also discover that the TLS or secure socket connection is terminated at the load balancer. So sometimes you'll see payment card data present on network equipment before it reaches the web server and then to the acquirer.

E-commerce

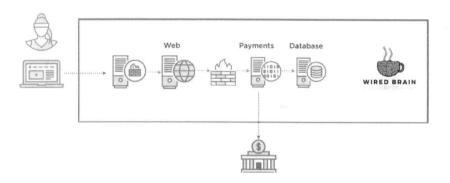

Many e-commerce merchants have a central payment system, so the customer's cardholder data goes from the web server, over an internal network, to a payment server or payment system, and from there to the acquirer. And of course, sometimes the merchant might do things like use encryption on their own internal network, so there are less places you could find cardholder data. In this example, I've shown that perhaps the cardholder data will be encrypted between the web server and the payment server, and so wouldn't pass through the internal firewall, and so if you looked there for cardholder data, you wouldn't see any. Other merchants also store a copy of the authorization data in a database, just in case. And so just as in a face-to-face transaction, in an e-commerce environment, there are lots of places you can find authorization data. It could be here on the firewall, here on the web server, it could be on internal networking equipment, it could be on a payment system, or it could even be in a database, and that's one of the reasons why working in payments is really interesting. Every merchant is different, and so it's always a discovery to find out where cardholder data might be. Now remember, we care about where authorization data is because a criminal can steal the authorization data themselves, and use it to make a transaction; however, stealing data is just a poor substitute for having the real card, and if at all possible, the PIN. Have you ever wondered what happens when an issuing bank or credit card company sends you a new payment card? Because criminals have, as they'd ideally like to steal real cards and PINs.

Making Payment Cards

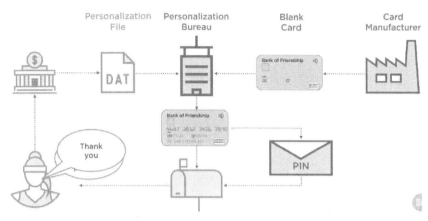

Now, let's imagine that for some reason Ann wants a new card. So she asks her issuing bank. The bank's prepared for this, as earlier in the year, it ordered lots of blank cards from a card manufacturer. The card manufacturer made blank physical cards with the bank's logo on it, and an programmed magnetic stripe and chip. It sent these to a company called the Personalization Bureau, which holds them securely for the bank. When Ann asks for a card, the bank includes Ann's details in a personalization file that it sends to the Personalization Bureau every day, which just basically contains all the cards we'd like you to make today. The Personalization Bureau takes the blank cards and the data sent from the bank, and on one card it puts Ann's name and programs the chip in the magnetic stripe. The Personalization Bureau often looks after postage and delivery of cards for the bank, so, they send it to Ann. If Ann also needs a PIN, the

Personalization Bureau will typically send this in the post, a few days after the card was sent. Sometimes you find that the card manufacturer and the Personalization Bureau are the same company. Now, criminals would love to be able to steal blank cards, and cards and PINs being sent from the bank or the bureau to the customer.

The Difference with Chip (EMV) Cards

Before we explore how the PCI standards protect card data from criminals, let's quickly discover the difference that chips make. Now, although much of the world has used cards with chips for a while, the USA has just started to implement them everywhere, and this is going to be great for data security. A few minutes ago, we saw how criminals could use stolen mag stripe data to make a clone card that the issuing bank wouldn't be able to tell apart from the real card. This is what the criminals did in some of those very large data breaches of cardholder data you might remember from 2014, such as Target, and Home Depot in the US, where track data was stolen from the retailer's point of sale systems, and used to make clone cards.

The Data on a Payment Card

Well, chip cards fixed that problem. The chip, or EMV chip which is its proper name, is increasingly found on cards. It's always in the same place, but it can look slightly different from one card to another, so some chips have got rounded corners, some have got cut off corners, some chips you'll see are gold, as opposed to silver, and it's not just the design on the card, it's actually a small computer that's powered up when the card is inserted into a chip-reading device, such as a point of interaction device, or as they tend to be called now, chip and PIN readers, or EMV readers, or even PIN entry devices or pads. They have lots of different names, but basically anything you insert the card into that reads the chip. So as well as the small computer, the chip contains some cryptographic secrets, and the way the chip uses those secrets is why criminals can't simply copy chip data and make a clone card, because unlike track data or the data on a magnetic stripe, the secret's never, ever leave the chip.

How an EMV Card Works

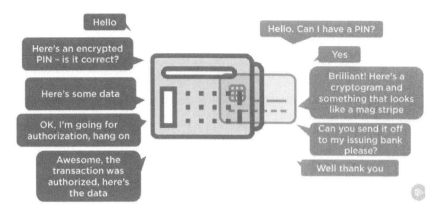

I'm going to simplify what happens in a face-to-face EMV transaction because the actual steps are quite complex, but basically, when an EMV terminal wants to make a transaction happen, it has a chat with the chip on the EVM card that's been inserted in it. First, the terminal and the chip say hello to each other. Part of the hello is working out how the rest of the transaction is going to work. For example, the chip might say to the terminal, oh by the way, I'm going to need a PIN for all transactions. The terminal then might ask the chip to validate the PIN that the user enters. In some parts of the world, the encrypted PIN is actually stored within the EMV chip, and so it can be validated without having to send it off to the issuer. So maybe next what happens is the terminal sends some data about the transaction to the chip. What data it sends differs between card schemes, but it will generally include some information about the merchant, like what the merchant does, and the amount of the transaction. Now here's the really clever part. The chip uses the unique cryptographic data that was stored in it at manufacture, and it generates a cryptographic signature, which is also called a cryptographic signature, which is also called a cryptogram, over the data sent by the terminal, and other data that the chip's got internally, and that will include, for instance, the identity of the merchant, and the amount of the transaction. And it generates this cryptogram, and it passes the cryptogram back to the terminal along with something that looks like a magnetic stripe, and it says to the terminal, please go and contact my issuing bank for authorization. So the terminal gets this data, and it sends the cryptogram and the pseudo-magnetic stripe data as an authorization request to the acquiring bank, and the acquiring bank's going to feed it through the payment system, and wait for the authorization response to come from the cardholder's issuing bank. And then when it gets the response back, the terminal passes the authorization response back to the card, and the transaction's completed.

EMV Authorization

WIRED BRAIN

Authorization Request

MagStripeImage | +Cryptogram | + Merchant ID, Name, $Amount

Response | Reference

Authorization Response

Ann's Bank

1. Validate mag stripe data
2. Generate cryptogram
3. Verify cryptograms match
4. Check balance

So with an EVM transaction, the authorization request consists of a pseudo-mag stripe track data read from the chip, the cryptogram generated by the chip, and the user information from the merchant about the transaction, the merchant's name and the amount of the transaction. Now, the issuer will check that the pseudo-mag stripe data is correct, just as it would for a mag stripe transaction, and the reason this mag stripe, it's called the mag stripe image or pseudo-mag stripe data, the reason this is in the system is when the world transitioned from mag stripe to chips, obviously lots of systems were expecting to see that Track 1 data, which is why it's still hanging around basically. So, first of all the issuing bank validates that mag stripe data, and then the next thing is, and this is really clever, the issuer generates the cryptogram itself, it knows the same cryptographic secret that the card knows, it's a secret that the issuing bank put into the card, and so what it does is it generates the cryptogram in the same way as the card generate the cryptogram, and it makes sure the cryptogram it generated matches the cryptogram that the card generated, because that means the only place that cryptogram could have been generated is on the card, and if they both match, it does the final check to see that Ann's got enough money in her accounts or enough credit, and then the transaction will be authorized.

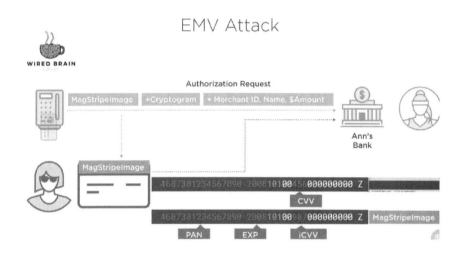

So let's see how a criminal can attack this transaction. Remember, the criminal wants to make a clone card from a data they steal. Well, the cryptographic sequence never leave the EVM chip, and so there's no data that can be stolen to make a clone chip card, but what about that pseudo-mag stripe data? Could the criminal use that to make a clone mag stripe card by taking the stolen data containing the pseudo- mag stripe image from the retailer's point of sale systems, and then writing it to a blank clone card? Well, you'll be pleased to know that the answer is no. The bank would recognize that. The reason is that the mag stripe image on the chip is actually different from the mag stripe on the back of the card. If you remember, the track data on a mag stripe card includes the three digits called the card verification value, or CVV, shown in red. Look, I'm just showing the Track 2 data here for clarity. Well, the mag stripe from the chip is a different three-digit value from the real mag stripe image, this is called the iCVV, and will always be a different value from the CVV encoded on the real mag stripe. So if a criminal steals the mag stripe image from an EMV chip card, and then they try to make a cloned mag stripe card using it, the issuing bank will notice it as being given the iCVV rather than the CVV attached to that card, and so it will refuse the transaction. So, I guess the question is, is it worth criminals stealing EVM transaction data? Well, it sort of is. The mag stripe image still includes the PAN and it still includes the expiration date, and this date could be used by criminals in e-commerce and MOTO to mail order and telephone orders.

Where the PCI Standards Come From

Criminals want:

1. Physical cards and PINs

2. Physical cards

3. Card data used to authorize transactions

- Magnetic stripe track data + PIN

- Magnetic stripe track data

- Ecommerce data

How do we stop them?

So far, we've established that in order of preference, criminals would most like to have physical cards and PINs, and if they can't have the PINs, then just physical cards, and if they can't have those, then they want to steal the data that could get a transaction authorized. So that's mag stripe data with a PIN, just mag stripe data, or data from an e-commerce transaction. So the question is how do we stop them?

Write a standard to tell people how to protect:

1. Physical cards and PINs

2. Physical cards

3. Card data used to authorize transactions

- Magnetic stripe track data + PIN

- Magnetic stripe track data

- Ecommerce data

Well, the answer is standards. If everyone in the world followed technical security standards that tell organizations how to protect physical cards, and PINs, and the card data used to authorize all types of transaction, then the criminals can be defeated; at least, that's how the card schemes believe they can stop majority of criminals, and so, each of the main card schemes, American Express, Discover, JCB, MasterCard, and Visa, have their own security standards for protecting data, for protecting PINs, and for protecting the production of cards. The standards told banks how to make sure that they're suppliers and the merchants took care of what the card schemes consider to be their data, to make sure that criminals could not take advantage of the card payment system. Now, having five different sets of security standards that actually sometimes used to contradict each other, was very confusing for the industry, and so in 2006, the Payment Card Industry Security Standards Council, or PCI SS, was formed.

Payment Card Industry Data Security Standard

PCI Payment Application Data Security Standard

PCI PIN Entry Device Security Standards

It was formed by the five card brands, American Express, Visa, MasterCard, Discover, and JCB, and they took the best bits out of each scheme's standards to make the PCI standards.

Criminals want cash and things they can trade for cash

They like physical cards and PINs

They also like authorization data

The card schemes' standards tell companies how to protect cards, PINs, and data from criminals

The card schemes created the PCI SSC to manage industry-wide standards

So let's have a quick recap. Before we take a look at the PCI standards, let's just quickly review what we've discovered so far. Criminals use card data to make money, either by taking money out of an ATM, or by buying things that they can then resell for money. They most like to steal physical cards and PINs, failing that, they want to steal the data that allows them to make a fraudulent transaction, and that's the data that's used when a transaction's authorized. The payment card schemes produced standards that tell people in the payment ecosystem, the acquiring banks, issuing banks, how the bank themselves and their supplies, and merchants, and merchant supplies must protect card data. The card schemes have their own standards, but in 2006, they agreed to create one entire set for the industry called the PCI standards.

There are basically five payment card industry standards. Depending on what you do, you might only come across one of them. I'm going to quickly go over all five so you can see how they fit together to protect all forms of cardholder data from criminals, and then we're going to look at each one in a bit more detail. So firstly, there's the Data Security Standard, or DSS, or PCI DSS, that protects cardholder data in organizations. Next, the Payment Application Data Security Standard, or PA-DSS, which helps people write secure software. Thirdly, a family of PIN Transaction Security Standards, PTS, which, as the name suggests, protects PINs. Next, a standard that strongly encrypts data between a point of interaction and where it's decrypted, called the Point-to-Point Encryption Standard, or P2PE, and finally, a standard that has no abbreviation or acronym, but a standard that secures the production and personalization of payment cards, the Card Production standard. Before we get into the details of all the PCI standards, I want to pause here for a second to say sorry, because we're about to enter an alphabet sea of the payment card industry, which is full of three-letter acronyms, and I know from experience, this can be quite confusing to begin with, especially when so many of the acronyms are really similar, and seem to have been chosen from a very limited set of letters, particularly P, Q, A, S, C, and I. But look, after a while, I promise this actually will become second nature to you.

PCI DSS and PCI PA-DSS

Payment Card Industry Data Security Standard PCI DSS	A standard to protect cardholder data
	Mostly logical controls
	Some physical controls
	Applies to organizations
	- Merchants
	- Service Providers

So let's start to look at the PCI standards with the most famous, and the one we all probably heard about: the Data Security Standard, or PCI DSS. It's a general information security standard with an emphasis on card data, and I know it's had its critics, but believe me, in 2006, this was an advanced data protection standard. It contains logical and physical controls, and applies to all organizations that store, process, or transmit cardholder data, including merchants, and third-parties that provide services to merchants, which in PCI terms, are called service providers. The PCI DSS standard consists of about 288 logical and physical security requirements that cover six main areas.

PCI DSS High Lε

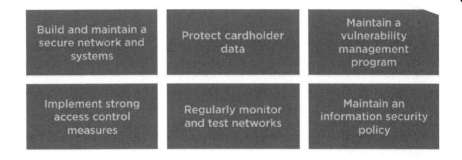

Build and maintain a secure network and systems	Protect cardholder data	Maintain a vulnerability management program
Implement strong access control measures	Regularly monitor and test networks	Maintain an information security policy

Firstly, building and maintaining secure networks, which contains requirements for installing and managing firewalls, along with system hardening, and the removal of default passwords, default services, and default security parameters. Second are requirements to protect cardholder data, typically by encryption, both in transit, when cardholder data is stored at rest. Third are an extensive set of requirements to develop software securely, patch and maintain developed and bought software, applications, and operating systems. Also the requirement to run effective, anti-virus software. Next are requirements that control the logical and physical access to cardholder data, including privileged access control, the use of IDs, passwords, and multifactor authentication. Fifth are equirements to have extensive logging and monitoring of the logs combined with vulnerability scanning and a penetration testing schedule. And finally, all this needs to be documented and understood by everyone in an organization that has responsibility for the protection of cardholder data. In all, PCI DSS contains those requirements across these six high-level areas. The requirements apply to all systems, people, and processes that store, process, or transmit cardholder data, and also systems that are connected to or could affect the security of cardholder data in the environment.

PCI Payment Application Data Security Standard PCI PA-DSS	A software development standard Intended for commercial, off-the-shelf, software Ensures software enables compliance with PCI DSS

Next, PCI DSS's best friend, which is PA-DSS. Now, you might have heard of this standard, but it's a software development standard designed for vendors that produce commercial software involved in the authorization or clearing of payment card transactions. The idea is that if a merchant buys software that's been validated to PA-DSS, they'll find it much easier to meet the requirements of PCI DSS. For example, one of the PCI DSS requirements is that passwords have to be over a certain length, and use a combination of characters. A PA-DSS validated application would allow passwords of that length, and with the complexity PCI DSS needs. So let's look at where PCI DSS and PA DSS apply in practice.

Which Standards Apply?

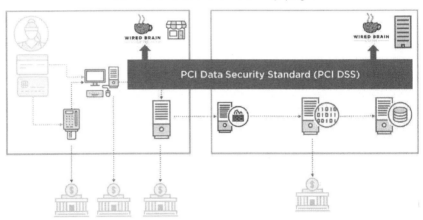

Now, you might remember this picture. It shows how payment card data may move around a face-to-face retail environment. Which of the PCI standards applies here? Well, Wired Brain Coffee stores, processes, and transmits cardholder data. So as an organization, you will have to protect that cardholder data by adhering to the requirements of PCI DSS. There's quite a subtle distinction here. It's the organization as a whole that has to comply with PCI DSS, it's not a component, a server, or some software, it's the whole company which has to ensure that any systems, processes, or people which store, process, and transmit cardholder data, meet the PCI DSS requirements.

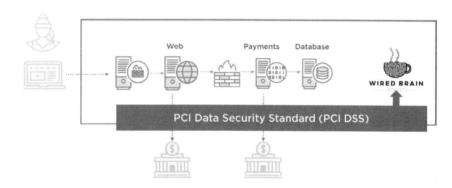

And if we take our e-commerce example, PCI DSS applies to the way that Wired Brain Coffee secures the cardholder data it receives from cardholders. Again, it's the organization that has to make sure that all its systems that can affect the security of cardholder data meet the PCI DSS requirements.

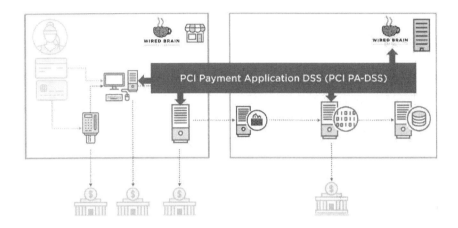

PA-DSS is a standard for companies that write software applications which are sold to merchants. It allows the software company to say that their software, if implemented correctly, will allow an organization to comply with the requirements of PCI DSS. It's really important to understand that just by buying software that's been validated to PA-DSS, it doesn't mean that the merchant that has bought the software automatically becomes compliant with PCI DSS. It's certainly going to help, but there are all the other requirements about PCI DSS, such as networking, antivirus, physical protection, logging, monitoring, and testing that the merchant also has to put in place. PCI DSS does not require a merchant to use PA-DSS validated software, but as I said earlier, it will help the merchant become compliant with PCI-DSS; however, some of the card schemes do require that merchants only buy PA-DSS validated applications. In this face-to-face retail example, any of the software used to process a payment on its way to authorization could have been built to comply with PA-DSS,

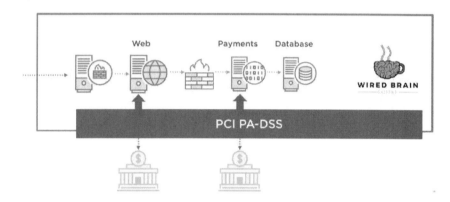

and in an e-com environment, Wired Brain Coffee could've bought a shopping cart of backend payment system off the shelf, and so this software could also be validated to comply with the PA-DSS requirements.

PIN Transaction Security Standards

PTS Standards

PTS is a family of standards that aim to protect cardholder PINs wherever they are processed. The first member of the family, PTS POI, or Point of Interaction, is concerned with the manufacturer and cryptographic key management of points of interaction, so that's any device that reads a card where the customer can enter their PIN. So this standard applies to physical hardware, the POI, and the firmware in it. It is usually the manufacturer of a device that gets their hardware tested against the standard, which covers things like tamper resistance, how the encryption keys that protect the PIN are secured internally, and how they're put into the device, and how the device is looked after from manufacturer to use. Making sure these devices are secure from the moment they are manufactured to when they're installed in a merchant is a real problem. Criminals have in the past compromised manufacturing facilities and the supply chain, so that when the devices were used, they kept a record of customer's card data and PINs, which the criminals then downloaded from the device and used themselves. The second, PCI PIN, is concerned with how organizations looked after the cryptographic keys used for PIN encryption and PIN decryption. That's mainly going to be issuers, acquirers, and other payment processors. So this standard is a bit like the DSS in that it contains a number of logical and physical controls that apply to how an organization manages security. The final PIN standard is one that you don't often come across, and is concerned with the security of Hardware Security Modules, or HSMs. These are typically used to manage and secure the cryptographic keys used to encrypt and decrypt PINs in banks and payment service providers, and like PTS POI, this is a standard that applies to physical hardware, the HSM, and the firmware in it. So that's the three members of the PTS family: Point of Interaction, PIN, and HSM. Let's see where they apply. The retail environment will contain devices where people enter their PIN. So these devices could be tested against PCI PTS POI, and remember, this isn't the merchant's responsibility, it's the manufacturer of a device that gets their hardware tested against the standard. All the merchant has to do is buy compliant devices, and whether a merchant has to use a compliant device or not is usually a condition that's put on them by their acquirer.

PTS in Practice

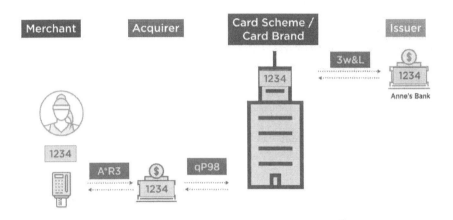

To see where PTS PIN may apply, let's see how a PIN moves between the entities in the payment system, and I am simplifying the process here just for clarity. So the cardholder enters a PIN on the PIN entry device, or the POI device in the merchant's coffee shop. The POI contains an encryption key placed there by the merchant's acquirer, which is used to encrypt the PIN. The encrypted PIN is sent to the acquirer, where it is decrypted and then re-encrypted using the card scheme's encryption key. The PIN is then sent to the scheme where it is once again decrypted and then re-encrypted with the issuer's encryption key. The scheme then sends the encrypted PIN to the issuer, where it's decrypted, and then checked against the PIN that the issuer has on file for the cardholder, and in this way, the merchant's point of interaction doesn't have to have the encryption keys for every single issuer in the world. So just as we saw in the first module how a payment card transaction moves from the merchant, through to the acquirer, to the card brand, and the issuer, the PIN does exactly the same thing, actually is part of the same authorization request, but because the PIN has to travel encrypted, it has to be encrypted and decrypted at each stage in the process, so the issuer can eventually decrypt it.

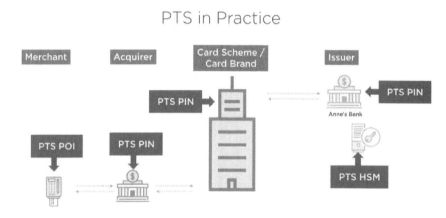

PTS in Practice

So it's obviously really important that the PIN and the keys used to encrypt and decrypt it protect it, and that's really the whole purpose of all the PTS standards. So as we know, PTS POI is considered the design, the manufacturer distribution, and management of the end user device is used in the merchants. PTS PIN describes the physical and logical controls for all the entities that do that encryption and decryption of PINs, so that's acquirers, card schemes, and issuers, and also payment processes. And finally, PTS HSM is a security standard for the hardware security modules that may be used to generate, store, encrypt, and decrypt PINs and PIN keys in acquirers, schemes, and issuers.

Simplification

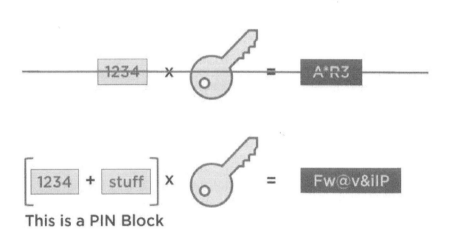

This is a PIN Block

Now, learning the intricacies of PTS and the three PTS standards would be a whole book in itself, but there's one simplification I made on the previous slide that I actually do need to expand on a little. So look, when a PIN is encrypted, it's not just a 4-digit or 32-bit PIN that's encrypted using the encryption key to produce a 4 character ciphertext. This would be too weak and it'd be easily broken. What happens is that the PIN is mathematically combined with some other data, actually, it's based on the primary account number and an Xorg operation to generate a 64-bit PIN block, and it's this PIN block that's encrypted using the PIN encryption key, and that's sufficiently long enough and much harder to break.

Point-to-point Encryption and Card Production Standards

So far, we've met PCI DSS, which applies to organizations that store, process, or transmit cardholder data. PA-DSS for commercial off the shelf software, and the PIN Transaction Security Standards that apply to all the areas where PIN is processed. Now let's take a quick look at the Point-to-Point Encryption Standard, or P2PE. The Point-to-Point Encryption Standard describes how to encrypt the primary account number in a POI device in the merchant's environments, and make sure it stays encrypted until it reaches a point of decryption, usually in a payment service provider or an acquirer. It specifies the physical and logical controls for key management, the security of the decryption environment, and also how the POI devices should be managed. The P2PE standard was developed so that merchants could buy solutions from service providers, and know the solution had been assessed to a high standard, and that cardholder data wouldn't be accessible in the merchant environments. Remember that when we looked at the face-to-face example earlier, there were lots of places you could potentially find authorization data: in devices, in electronic cash registers, in point of sale systems, in store servers, and in servers in a head office. Well, the goal of the Point-to-Point Encryption Standard is to make sure that all cardholder data in the merchant environment is strongly encrypted, and so useless to criminals.

P2PE

It does this very much in the way that PINs are encrypted, by strongly encrypting the PAN in the PTS POI device, using an encryption key supplied by the acquirer, or a payment processor, or a service provider. The data flowing through the merchant systems is now encrypted, and so the criminal won't be able to get cardholder data from the merchant environments, and of course nothing in the merchant's environment now stores, processes, or transmits unencrypted cardholder data, and so the PCI DSS requirements won't apply to the majority of systems in the merchant environments, which is really cost-effective for the merchant. The merchant doesn't have to apply those 288 controls to every device in the merchant environment. There is a downside. Using P2PE means the merchant won't be able to retain cardholder data, for example, in a database like they used to. The final payment card industry standard we're going to meet is the payment card production standard or card production standard. Unlike the other standards, actually this one doesn't have an abbreviation, so I'm going to keep calling it card production. It's a set of physical and logical standards that describe the security around how cards are manufactured, personalized, and distributed, and also how PINs are sent to cardholders. This standard is actually split into two documents: one for physical controls, and the other for logical controls, and because it's concerned with looking at the payment cards in bulk, they're actually a lot more physical security requirements than you normally see in an information security standard. It's actually a really interesting read if you normally just do logical security and you haven't see a whole lot of physical security.

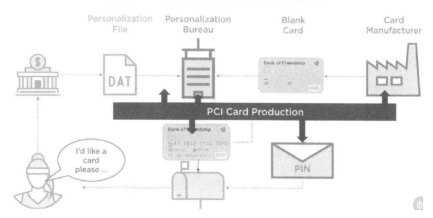

So, looking back at our example of how a card and PIN is made for a customer, the PCI Card Production standards will apply to manufacturers, the personalization bureau, how the personalization bureau receives data from the issuer, how the card, and how the PIN are sent to the cardholder. If all the entities involved in card production comply with the standard, the idea is it will stop criminals from stealing cards and PINs from the manufacturing and distribution process, which will actually be really damaging for the industry because you'd have this problem that you didn't actually know that cards were manufactured in a secure manner. To date, this is a really successful standard, it's only recently become a PCI standard, it used to be an individual scheme standard, and only recently has it been merged together, the MasterCard scheme and the Visa scheme to actually make it a PCI standard.

Where to Find the Payment Card Industry Standards

So there we are. We met the five main PCI standards to aim to stop criminals from stealing cards, PINs, and card data. Firstly, the Data Security Standard, PCI DSS. Secondly, the Payment Application Data Security Standard, PA-DSS. Thirdly, the three standards that make up the PIN Transaction Standards, PIN, HSM, and probably most importantly, the standard that applies to terminals where you enter your PIN, the Point of Interaction Standard. Next, the Point-to-Point Encryption Standard, P2PE, and finally, the two Card Production standards, the logical and the physical security requirements for card production. As you can see, all these standards are actually available as PDF documents, you can get them all from the PCI SSC website. They're free, unlike ISO Standards, you don't have to pay for them, you can just download any of them from the document library. There is a click-through license agreement you have to agree to when you click on any of them, but read that, click I Agree at the bottom, and then you can just download the standard, but again, you don't pay anybody for them.

What Criminals Want

They steal this:	To:
Cards (±PINs)	Withdraw money from ATMs Buy goods
Magstripe (track) data (±PIN)	Make clone magstripe cards +PIN = ATMs -PIN = buy goods
Ecommerce data (PAN, Exp, ±CVV2)	Buy goods that they can turn into cash at other Ecommerce merchants
Chip Data MSI (PAN, Exp)	Buy goods that they can turn into cash at other Ecommerce merchants that do not ask for CVV2

So, let's remind ourselves of the data that criminals want and the data that the standards are protecting. So criminals want to steal cards, they want to steal cards ideally with PINs, so they can take money from ATMs, and go to stores and buy goods. If they can't steal cards, they like to steal mag stripe data, and with mag stripe data, they can make clone mag stripe cards, if they've got the PIN they can go through an ATM, if they haven't got the PIN, they can go to stores, buy goods, and sell those goods for cash. If they can't get mag stripe data or cards, they like e-commerce data, the primary account number, the expiration date, and ideally the CVV2, and then they'll go to other e-com shops and they'll buy goods that they can turn into cash. And then finally, if they can't get any of that, they'll take the mag stripe image data from a chip transaction because it's going to have the primary account number and expiration date in it, and then again, they'll go shopping at e-com merchants that don't ask for the CVV2 code.

Criminals want physical cards and data so they can make money

It's mostly the authorization messages that contain the data that criminals want

The PCI Standards help organizations to protect cardholder data from criminals by specifying logical and physical security requirements

PCI DSS cardholder data
PCI PA-DSS software
PCI PTS PIN | POI | HSM PIN security
PCI P2PE encrypting cardholder data
PCI Card Production manufacturing and personalization

Remember, the only reason that criminals target cards and card data is financial; they could turn that data into money. It's the authorization messages that are the most valuable, but if everyone protects cardholder data by following the relevant PCI standards, then it makes the criminal's job much harder, and those standards are PCI DSS to protect cardholder data, PA-DSS for off the shelf software, PTS standards for protecting PINs, the P2PE standard for encrypting cardholder data in a return environment, and then finally the Card Production standards that apply to the manufacturing and personalization of cards. If everyone follows those standards, it'll make the criminal's lives much harder.

Printed in Great Britain
by Amazon